Contents

Health is good!

It's good
to be healthy.

When we are healthy,
we have lots of energy.

A Sense of Science

Exploring Health

FRANKLIN WATTS
LONDON • SYDNEY

3900

First published in 2007 by
Franklin Watts
338 Euston Road
London NW1 3BH

Franklin Watts Australia
Level 17/207 Kent Street
Sydney NSW 2000

Editor: Jeremy Smith
Art Director: Jonathan Hair
Design: Matthew Lilly
Cover and design
concept:
Jonathan Hair

Photograph credits:
Steve Shott except: Alamy:
15b, 21b, 22, 23b. Corbis:
19. istockphoto: 6, 12,
13, 15t, 25.

A CIP catalogue record
for this book is available
from the British Library.

Dewey classification: 613

ISBN 978 0 7496 7044 3

Printed in China

Franklin Watts is a division of
Hachette Children's Books.

We can think hard.

Skip to it!

How many
times can you
skip in one
minute? Now try
and beat
your score.

We have a
good appetite!

Food and health

The food we eat helps us to stay healthy.

Egg

Cheese

Meat

Some foods help our body to grow.

Some foods give us energy.

Rice

Potato

Bread

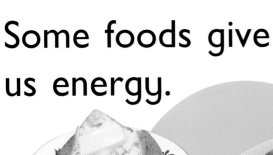

Taste it

Close your eyes and ask a friend to feed you different kinds of fruit. Can you tell what each one is?

Some foods help us to fight sickness.

Fruit

Vegetables

Eating well

To be healthy, we need to eat many different foods.

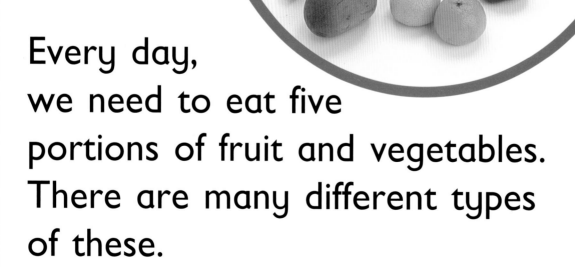

Every day, we need to eat five portions of fruit and vegetables. There are many different types of these.

Try not to eat too much sugary food. It's good for a special treat.

Water is good for the body. It is much better for you than sugary drinks.

Glug, glug

Measure how much water you drink every day. Would it fill a glass, a jug or a bucket?

Exercise

Exercise helps us to stay healthy.

When we work our body, we make it stronger.

In and out

When we breathe, we use our lungs. Take a deep breath in and out. Which parts of the body move?

Running around is good for our muscles and bones.

Exercise is good for our heart and lungs.

Keep active!

We can exercise our body in all sorts of ways.

J-J-J-Jump!
Jump up and down for a minute. Stop. What changes do you notice in your body?

We can walk instead of ride in a car.

We can play
outside instead of
watching TV.

It's fun to be active with friends.

All about germs

Germs are tiny things that live on our bodies. Some of them can make us ill.

Hair test
Examine your hair before and after washing. What do you notice about the way it looks and feels?

To stay healthy, we need to wash them away!

We can brush away the germs that rot our teeth.

Wash cuts and cover them to keep germs out.

Stop germs spreading

Germs can spread easily and make lots of people ill.

It takes time to wash your hands well. Sing the whole verse of 'Happy Birthday' while you rub them with soap.

Stop germs spreading by washing your hands when you have been to the toilet.

Catch germs in a tissue when you sneeze.

Wash your hands after touching a pet.

Germs and food

Some germs can spoil our food.

Bad food tastes nasty and can make us ill.

Nice or nasty?

Put a piece of bread in a plastic bag and leave it somewhere warm for a few days. What happens to it?

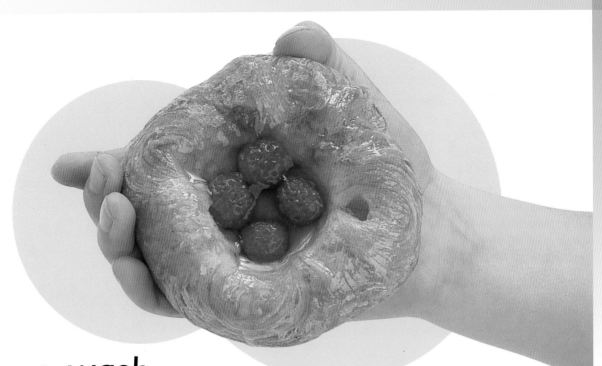

Always wash your hands before touching food.

Flies spread germs. Never let them land on your food.

Sun care

To be healthy,
we need to take care
in the sun.

Wearing a T-shirt and a sunhat helps
to protect our skin.

Sun cream helps
to stop our skin
burning.

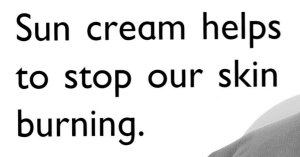

Stay in the
shade in the
middle of
the day.

Sun or shade
On a summer's day, stand in the shade
for a minute, then go out into the sun.
Do you notice any difference?

Medicines

Doctors give us medicines to make us better when we are ill.

Nice or nasty?
When were you last given a medicine? What did it taste like?

Never take medicines on your own.

Medicines are very strong and we only need a little.

We keep medicines in a safe place.

Some medicines look like sweets but they can be dangerous. Never eat them.

Only take medicines given to you by an adult.

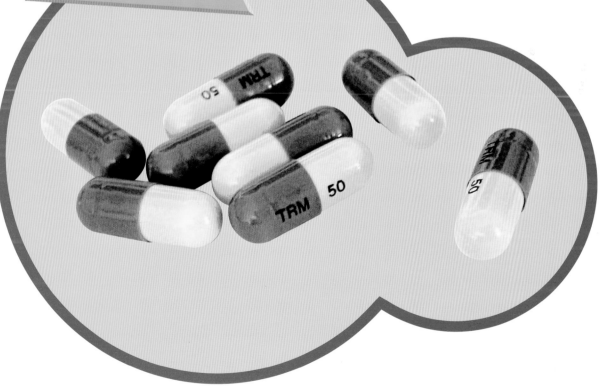

A good sleep

At the end of the day our bodies need to rest.

We sleep all night long.

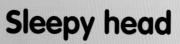

Sleepy head

How do you know when you are tired?
What do you feel like doing then?

Rest and sleep help to make us better when we feeling ill.

Sleep gives us energy for the day ahead.

Glossary

Appetite
Wanting food because you feel hungry.

Bones
The hard parts inside the body.

Energy
A feeling of get-up-and-go.

Exercise
Activity for the body.

Germs
Tiny living things that spread sickness.

Healthy
To be fit and well.

Heart
The part of your body that pumps blood around.

Lungs
The parts of the body that help you to breathe.

Muscles
The parts of the body that help you to move.

Portion
A helping of food.

Make a fruit kebab

1. Choose three fruits that you like to eat – for example banana, kiwis and satsumas.

2. With a grown-up, wash, peel and slice the fruit.

3. Thread the fruit onto some wooden skewers or cocktail sticks, one piece at a time. Eat and enjoy!

Index